ABCs of Animal Dances

Written and Illustrated by Vanessa Salgado
with Donna Salgado

© 2014 Crafterina. All Rights Reserved.
Published by Crafterina
ISBN 978-0-9886652-2-4
www.Crafterina.com

Arching Alligator

Bird Balance

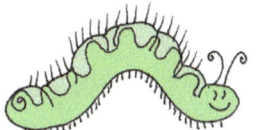 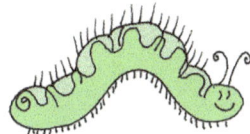 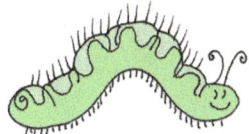

Caterpillar Crawl

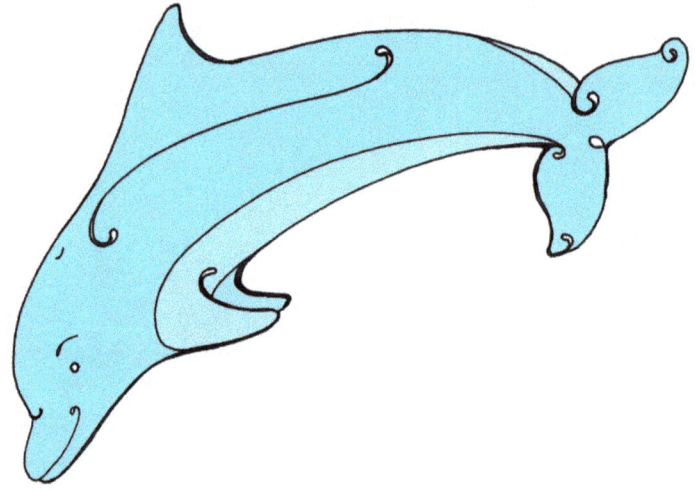

Diving Dolphin

Elephant Extensions

Flying Firefly

Galloping Giraffe

H are Hops

Insect Isolations

Jumping Jaguar

Kicking Kitten

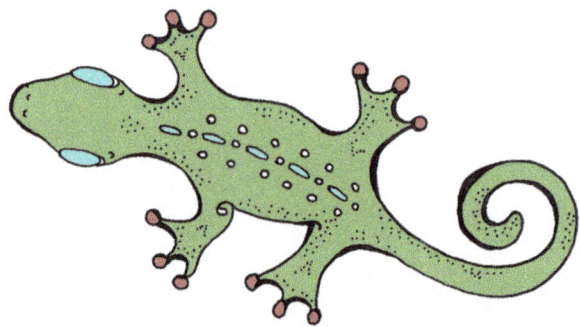

Leaping Lizard

Migrating Monarch

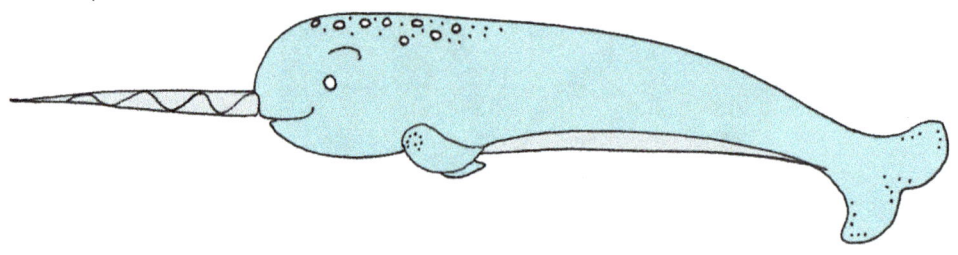

Noodling Narwhal

O pen-armed Orangutan

Posing Penguin

Quick Queen Bee

Rolling River Otter

Slow Snail

Tip-toeing Tarantula

Upright Unicorn

Vibrating Vulture

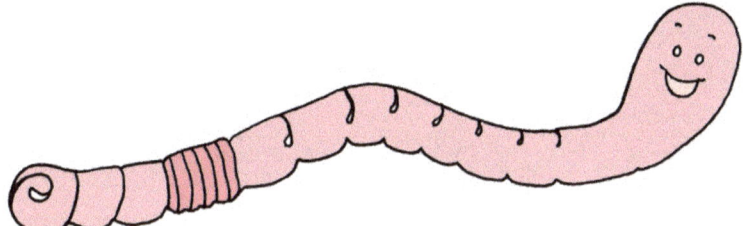

Wiggle Worm

eXpressive X-Ray Fish

Yoga-ing Yellow Lab

Zig-zag Zebra

 Arching Alligator

 Bird Balance

 Caterpillar Crawl

 Diving Dolphin

 Elephant Extensions

 Flying Firefly

 Galloping Giraffe

 Hare Hops

 Insect Isolations

 Jumping Jaguar

 Kicking Kitten

 Leaping Lizard

 Migrating Monarch

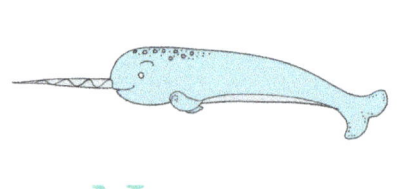
Noodling Narwhal

Open-armed Orangutan

Posing Penguin

Quick Queen Bee

Rolling River Otter

Slow Snail

Tip-toeing Tarantula

Upright Unicorn

Vibrating Vulture

Wiggle Worm

E**X**pressive X-Ray Fish

Yoga-ing Yellow Lab

Zig-zag Zebra

About the Author and Illustrator:

Vanessa Salgado is a Professional Dancer and Visual Artist based out of New York City. She has taught creative movement and foundational ballet classes to many little dancers throughout Manhattan.

Vanessa is a graduate of the world famous Alvin Ailey/Fordham University BFA Program at Lincoln Center. She also holds a Certification in Dance Education from the Dance Education Laboratory at the NY 92nd St. Y Harkness Dance Center.

Her earliest memories involve story time with her dad, creating with her mom after school, and attending weekend ballet class alongside her sister, Donna.

Her interests in visual art revealed themselves wholeheartedly in high school as she simultaneously trained vigorously for the professional dance world. As she transitioned into her college days and now into her professional life, her incessant doodles and crafting have remained a source of wonder for all those around her.

For more information about Vanessa, please visit www.VanessaSalgado.com.
Please visit www.Crafterina.com for children's crafts and dance resources.

www.Crafterina.com
© Crafterina. All Rights Reserved.

www.ingramcontent.com/pod-product-compliance
Lightning Source LLC
Chambersburg PA
CBHW040731020526
44112CB00058B/2933